200 juice diet recipes

hamlyn | all colour cookbook

200 juice diet recipes

Joy Skipper

An Hachette UK Company
www.hachette.co.uk

First published in Great Britain in 2015 by Hamlyn
a division of Octopus Publishing Group Ltd
Endeavour House, 189 Shaftesbury Avenue
London WC2H 8JY
www.octopusbooks.co.uk

ISBN: 978-0-60063-054-8

A CIP catalogue record for this book is available from the
British Library

Printed and bound in China

10 9 8 7 6 5 4 3 2 1

Both metric and imperial measurements have
been given in all recipes. Use one set of measurements
only, and not a mixture of both.

Standard level spoon measurements are used in all recipes
1 tablespoon = 15 ml spoon
1 teaspoon = 5 ml spoon

200 ml (7 fl oz) makes one average serving.

Ovens should be preheated to the specified temperature –
if using a fan-assisted oven, follow the manufacturer's
instructions for adjusting the time and temperature.

Fresh herbs should be used unless otherwise stated.
Freshly ground black pepper should be used unless
otherwise stated.

This book includes dishes made with nuts and nut
derivatives. It is advisable for people with known allergic
reactions to nuts and nut derivatives or those who may be
potentially vulnerable to these allergies, such as pregnant
and nursing mothers, invalids, the elderly, babies and
children, to avoid dishes made with these. It is prudent to
check the labels of all pre-prepared ingredients for the
possible inclusion of nut derivatives.

Before making any changes to your diet and health regime,
always consult a doctor.

contents

introduction

introduction

juicing for diet

One of the easiest ways to improve the nutritional content of your meals is to include juices in your daily diet.

Lots of important vitamins and minerals are found in the fibrous parts of fruit and vegetables and getting a big hit of those vitamins and minerals would mean eating an enormous amount of food. Could you eat two beetroot, one orange, one apple, half a cucumber and a wedge of cabbage all in one sitting? No, but you could drink their juice. Juicing releases all the nutrients from those ingredients so that they can be easily absorbed into the bloodstream. We are constantly told to eat more fruit and vegetables, but while eating a large plate of kale for its nutritional content is hard work, drinking it in a juice with other great-tasting vegetables and fruits is really very easy.

Making juices from scratch ensures they are fresh and it's important to drink them pretty quickly. Once foods have been juiced the enzymes in the food continue to break down the molecules of food into smaller particles, making the juices easy to digest but with fewer nutrients as time goes by. These enzymes are responsible for hundreds of chemical reactions taking place in our bodies, so including them in our diet is hugely important.

By drinking fresh juices you help the digestive process, which for a lot of people can be sluggish, and this in turn means you are more likely to absorb all the great nutrients you consume, which go on to support the other systems throughout your body.

which juicer?

There are two different types of juicer available:

- **Centrifugal** – these are the most common

type of juicer, using a fast-spinning metal blade that spins against a mesh filter, separating juice from flesh via centrifugal force.

• **Masticating** – these juicers extract juice by first crushing and then pressing fruit and vegetables for the highest possible yield.

There are a lot of different models to choose from, so before you rush out to buy one you need to consider the following questions:

- How easy is it to clean the juicer?
- How small do you have to chop your ingredients?
- How effective is the juicer?
- How much do you want to spend?
- What do you want to juice? If, for instance, you want to juice wheatgrass, only a masticating juicer will do this.

juicing tips

- As with all food preparation, it's good to be organized, so make sure you have all the ingredients to hand before you start.
- The size of the funnel of your juicer will dictate how small you need to chop your ingredients. This is something to take into account when you are choosing your juicer. If the funnel is large enough, you may not need to chop some fruit or vegetables at all.
- Fill the funnel before starting the juicer and keep the machine running for 15–20 seconds after you have finished juicing. You will be surprised how much juice continues to run out.
- You have to peel ingredients that have thick skin, such as kiwifruit, pineapples

and fresh root ginger. Citrus fruits can be peeled or not, it's entirely up to you.

- If you are juicing lots of leaves, such as spinach or watercress, it's good to add these to the juicer in between more solid ingredients, such as apples or carrots, to help them to be pressed into the juicer.
- As you will be using the peel of lots of ingredients, be sure to wash the fruit and vegetables thoroughly; even if they are organic they could still be contaminated with bacteria.
- Wash the juicer immediately after juicing. If you leave it too long, the pulp will harden and be difficult to remove.

juicing for health

Fruit juices have received a lot of bad press over the past few years, claiming that they are full of sugar and should be consumed in moderation. Well, this is the case for most foods: everything should be consumed in moderation, so keep this in mind when juicing every day.

If you have a sweet tooth or are borderline diabetic, sticking to vegetable juices would be more beneficial for you. If you don't like vegetables, then this is a great way for you to include them in your diet. You will be surprised how sweet the vegetable juices can be (*see* pages 16–69).

Be aware that drinking too many fruit juices can increase your calorie intake: one small juice could contain three or four whole fruits, so choosing vegetable juices is preferable.

When you juice fruit and vegetables you remove the fibre, which is necessary for a healthy diet, so it's very important to replace the fibre with ingredients such as ground chia seeds or ground linseeds. Alternatively, you could use the pulp from the juicer to make soups or muffins, for example.

juicing for weight loss

When most people try to lose weight they cut down on lots of foods, some of which could actually aid weight loss. Reducing

Foods that support the liver

- Garlic
- Grapefruit
- Beetroot
- Leafy green vegetables
- Avocado
- Cold-pressed oils, such as avocado, flaxseed and hemp
- Cruciferous vegetables, such as cabbage and broccoli
- Lemons and limes
- Walnuts
- Turmeric

calories tends to mean you are reducing the nutrients that your body needs to run your busy lifestyle. That's where juicing comes in.

There are a number of nutrients that are very important when trying to lose weight, mostly those nutrients that support your digestive system (helping you to digest foods and absorb nutrients) and your liver (supporting the detoxification process and getting rid of waste). When you lose weight you start to lose the toxins that are stored in the fat cells, which gives your liver extra work to do, so supporting the liver at this time is beneficial to your health.

Foods that aid digestion

- Yogurt
- Fish oils
- Ginger
- Pineapple
- Peppermint

is it necessary to fast on juices alone? Fasting is one way that a lot of people like to start dieting, just because it gives them a boost of confidence when the first weight drops off, but long-term weight loss should be slow and more controlled. Using juices, smoothies, dips or soups as meal replacements is a better option: the slower you lose weight, the more likely you are to keep it off and not suffer from headaches and withdrawal symptoms while you are doing it. It's also easier to stick to replacing the odd meal than it is to try to fast when you have a busy lifestyle.

Juicing fruit and vegetables is only part of the picture with regards to weight loss: your diet still needs to include both protein and fat.

Protein is needed for muscle repair and can be found in lean meats, fish, eggs, lentils and beans, and dairy products. Fat is needed for healthy cells all over the body, including the brain, and good fats are known to help remove bad fats so you should still include oily fish (such as salmon and mackerel), avocados and nuts in your diet.

juice diet tips

- Use raw, organic vegetables and fruit wherever possible – to avoid toxins going into your body you need to eat 'clean' foods.

- Limit the number of fruit juices you have each day; choose vegetable juices instead.

- Add protein and fat to your diet by adding chia seeds, linseeds, avocado oil, protein powder and green powders, such as wheatgrass, spirulina and chlorella, to your juices or smoothies.

- Don't drink the same juice every day. As with your normal diet, the more variety, the more nutrients you are likely to absorb. Although you have a huge number of recipes to choose from in this book, also experiment with your own combinations of fruit and vegetables.

what about exercise?

Studies have shown that people who lose weight gradually will be able to maintain their weight better with regular exercise. This doesn't mean you need to join a gym. If you've never exercised before, one of the best forms of exercise is walking. Just start to walk for 20 minutes, 3 times a week, then gradually increase this as you feel you can. When you get to the point that you want more exercise, talk to a personal trainer or ask your local gym for more advice.

vegetable
juices

citrus beet juice

Makes **about 400 ml
(14 fl oz)**

1 **orange**, about 160 g
  (5½ oz)
1 **beetroot**, about 125 g
  (4 oz)
1 large **carrot**, about 150 g
  (5 oz), plus extra to decorate
½ **cucumber**, about 175 g
  (6 oz)

Roughly peel the orange. Juice the orange with
the beetroot, carrot and cucumber.

Pour the juice into a glass, decorate with slices of carrot
and serve immediately.

For spicy citrus beet juice, follow the recipe above,
adding a 2 cm (¾ inch) piece peeled fresh root ginger
to the juicer with the other ingredients.

mean green juice

Makes **about 450 ml**
  (¾ pint)

1 **apple**, about 125 g (4 oz)
¹/₃ **cucumber**, about 100 g
  (3½ oz)
2 **celery sticks**, plus extra to
  decorate
30 g (1¼ oz) **kale**
1 **lemon**
15 g (½ oz) **parsley**
1 teaspoon **wheatgrass
  powder**
ice cubes

Juice the apple with the cucumber, celery, kale, lemon and parsley. Whisk in the wheatgrass powder.

Pour the juice into a glass over ice, add a trimmed celery stick and serve immediately.

For sweet mean green juice, replace the kale with an extra apple – about 125 g (4 oz) – and 1 orange – about 160 g (5½ oz) – and juice as above.

heart beet juice

Makes **about 350 ml**
   (12 fl oz)

1 **orange**, about 160 g
   (5½ oz)
1 **beetroot**, about 125 g
   (4 oz)
1 **apple**, about 125 g (4 oz)
ice cubes

Grate the rind of the orange onto a plate. Roughly peel the orange and cut into wedges. Rub the rim of a glass with a wedge of orange, then dip the rim of the glass into the grated orange rind to coat the rim.

Juice together the orange wedges, beetroot and apple.

Pour the juice into the prepared glass over ice and serve immediately.

For green heart beet juice, follow the recipe above, adding 50 g (2 oz) spinach to the juicer with the other ingredients.

fabulous fennel juice

Makes **about 300 ml**
  (½ pint)

1 **fennel bulb**, about 150 g
  (5 oz)
1 **apple**, about 100 g (3½ oz)
1 **carrot**, about 150 g (5 oz)
grated **nutmeg**, to sprinkle

Juice all the ingredients together.

Pour the juice into a glass, sprinkle with a large pinch of nutmeg and serve immediately.

For fennel & orange juice, roughly peel 1 orange – about 160 g (5½ oz). Juice the orange with 1 fennel bulb – about 150 g (5 oz) – and 1 carrot – about 150 g (5 oz). To add extra fibre to the juice, if desired, stir in ½ teaspoon ground linseeds.

tropical green juice

Makes **about 350 ml (12 fl oz)**

1 slice **pineapple**, about 180 g (6¼ oz)
50 g (2 oz) **kale**
20 g (¾ oz) **spinach**
1 **apple**, about 125 g (4 oz)
1 teaspoon **green powder** (such as wheatgrass, spirulina or chlorella)
ice cubes

Roughly peel the pineapple. Juice the pineapple with the kale, spinach and apple. Stir in the green powder and mix well.

Pour the juice into a glass over ice and serve immediately.

For sweet & hot tropical green juice, replace the spinach with 1 large carrot – about 150 g (5 oz) – and juice as above. Stir in a few drops of Tabasco sauce with the green powder and serve poured over ice.

sweet pepper juice

Makes **about 250 ml**
  (8 fl oz)

1 teaspoon ground **mixed**
  peppercorns
lime wedge
1 **red pepper**, about 175 g
  (6 oz)
20 **red grapes**
2–3 **ice cubes**

Place the ground peppercorns on a small plate. Rub the rim of a glass with the lime wedge and dip the rim of the glass into the peppercorns to coat the rim.

Core and deseed the red pepper. Juice the pepper with the grapes.

Transfer the juice to a food processor or blender, add the ice cubes and process briefly until smooth.

Pour the juice into the prepared glass and serve immediately.

For hot sweet pepper juice, core and deseed 1 red pepper – about 175 g (6 oz). Juice the pepper with 1 apple – about 100 g (3½ oz) – and a 2 cm (¾ inch) piece peeled fresh root ginger. Serve with a dash of Tabasco sauce.

kick start juice

Makes **about 350 ml (12 fl oz)**

1 **lemon**
2 cm (¾ inch) piece fresh **root ginger**
1 **garlic clove**
1 **apple**, about 100 g (3½ oz)
1 **carrot**, about 150 g (5 oz)
2 **celery sticks**
100 g (3½ oz) **alfalfa sprouts**

Roughly peel the lemon, ginger and garlic. Juice all the ingredients together.

Pour the juice into a glass and serve immediately.

For clean start juice, juice 1 roughly peeled lemon with 1 roughly peeled lime, ½ cucumber – about 175 g (6 oz) – and a 2 cm (¾ inch) piece peeled fresh root ginger. Pour the juice into a tall glass and top up with sparkling water.

popeye power juice

Makes **about 250 ml (8 fl oz)**

60 g (2¼ oz) **spinach**
2 **celery sticks**
1 **apple**, about 100 g (3½ oz)

Juice all the ingredients together.

Pour the juice into a glass and serve immediately.

For extra Popeye power juice, juice the spinach, celery and apple as above, then stir in ½ teaspoon green powder and 1 teaspoon avocado oil and serve.

spicy beet juice

Makes **about 250 ml (8 fl oz)**

1 large **beetroot**, about 175 g (6 oz)
15 g (½ oz) **coriander leaves**
2 **celery sticks**
large pinch of ground **turmeric**
pepper

Juice the beetroot with the coriander and celery. Whisk in the ground turmeric. Season the juice to taste with pepper.

Pour the juice into a glass and serve immediately.

For spicy roots juice, juice 1 parsnip – about 100 g (3½ oz), 1 carrot – about 150 g (5 oz), 1 apple – about 100 g (3½ oz) – and a 2 cm (¾ inch) piece peeled fresh root ginger. Whisk in large pinch of ground turmeric and serve.

carrot juice

Makes **about 300 ml**
  (½ pint)

1 **lemon**
1 **carrot**, about 150 g (5 oz)
2 **Little Gem lettuces**, about
  275 g (9 oz) in total
1 **apple**, about 100 g (3½ oz)
1 teaspoon **chia oil**

Grate the lemon rind and reserve. Roughly peel the lemon. Juice the lemon with the carrot, lettuce and apple. Stir in the reserved grated lemon rind and chia oil.

Pour the juice into a glass and serve immediately.

For stinging carrot juice, roughly peel 1 lemon. Juice the lemon with 2 carrots – about 300 g (10 oz) in total, 1 apple – about 100 g (3½ oz) – and a handful of stinging nettles.

healing green juice

Makes **about 450 ml
(¾ pint)**

40 g (1½ oz) **kale**
30 g (1¼ oz) **spinach**
1 **Little Gem lettuce,** about
140 g (4½ oz)
2 **celery sticks**
½ **cucumber,** about 175 g
(6 oz)
1 **apple,** about 100 g (3½ oz)
½ teaspoon **spirulina powder**
1 teaspoon **hemp seed oil**
ice cubes

Juice the kale with the spinach, lettuce, celery,
cucumber and apple. Stir in the spirulina powder
and hemp seed oil.

Pour the juice into a glass over ice and serve
immediately.

For healing beet juice, juice 40 g (1½ oz) kale with
½ cucumber – about 175 g (6 oz), 1 beetroot – about
150 g (5 oz), 1 apple – about 100 g (3½ oz) – and a
2 cm (¾ inch) piece peeled fresh root ginger. Stir in
½ teaspoon chlorella powder. Serve poured over ice.

purple power juice

Makes **about 300 ml**
  (½ pint)

2 cm (¾ inch) piece fresh **root
  ginger**
100 g (3½ oz) **red cabbage**
1 **celery stick**
1 **apple**, about 100 g (3½ oz)
12 **red grapes**
ice cubes

Peel the ginger. Juice together the peeled ginger, cabbage, celery, apple and grapes.

Pour the juice into a glass over ice and serve immediately.

For purple protein juice, juice 100 g (3½ oz) red cabbage with 12 red grapes, 1 beetroot – about 125 g (4 oz) – and 2 carrots – about 300 g (10 oz) in total. Whisk in 1 tablespoon protein powder and serve.

vitamin c punch

Makes **about 250 ml
(8 fl oz)**

2 **lemons**
1 cm (½ inch) piece fresh
  horseradish root
1 **apple**, about 100 g (3½ oz)
15 g (½ oz) **parsley**

Roughly peel the lemons. Juice all the ingredients together.

Pour the juice into a glass and serve immediately.

For spicy lemon tea, juice 2 roughly peeled lemons and a 1 cm (½ inch) piece fresh horseradish root, pour into a cup and top up with boiling water.

minty summer juice

Makes **about 300 ml (½ pint)**

6 **asparagus spears**
½ **cucumber**, about 175 g (6 oz)
2 young **carrots**, about 200 g (7 oz)
small handful of **mint**, plus an extra mint sprig to decorate
ice cubes

Juice together the asparagus, cucumber, carrots and mint.

Pour the juice into a glass over ice, top with a sprig of mint and serve immediately.

For spicy summer juice, juice 6 asparagus spears with ½ cucumber – about 175 g (6 oz), 1 apple – about 100 g (3½ oz) – and a 2 cm (¾ inch) piece peeled fresh root ginger.

boost juice

Makes **about 400 ml (14 fl oz)**

1 **pomegranate**, about 250 g (8 oz)
1 **apple**, about 100 g (3½ oz)
1 **orange**, about 200 g (7 oz)
2 **carrots**, about 300 g (10 oz) in total
25 g (1 oz) **radish sprouts**

Remove the seeds from the pomegranate by cutting the fruit in half, then holding the halved fruit over a bowl and hitting the skin with a wooden spoon so that the seeds fall into the bowl. Juice all the ingredients together.

Pour the juice into a glass and serve immediately.

For spicy boost juice, juice 1 orange – about 200 g (7 oz) – with 1 apple – about 100 g (3½ oz), 2 carrots – about 300 g (10 oz) in total, 25 g (1 oz) radish sprouts and ½ red chilli. Season with black pepper and serve.

beet treat juice

Makes **about 350 ml**
(12 fl oz)

1 slice **pineapple**, about
100 g (3½ oz), plus a
pineapple wedge to decorate
1 **orange**, about 200 g (7 oz)
2 **beetroot**, about 300 g
(10 oz) in total
100 g (3½ oz) **red cabbage**

Roughly peel the pineapple and the orange. Juice all the ingredients together.

Pour the juice into a glass, decorate with a wedge of pineapple and serve immediately.

For sweet beet treat juice, juice 2 beetroot – about 300 g (10 oz) in total, with 2 oranges – about 400 g (13 oz) in total, 1 slice roughly peeled pineapple – about 100 g (3½ oz) – and 2 peeled kiwifruit.

beautiful brussels juice

Makes **about 300 ml**
 (½ pint)

2 cm (¾ inch) piece fresh
 root ginger
6 **Brussels sprouts**
1 **carrot**, about 150 g (5 oz)
1 **apple**, about 100 g (3½ oz)

Peel the ginger. Juice all the ingredients together.

Pour the juice into a glass and serve immediately.

For bountiful Brussels juice, juice 10 Brussels sprouts with 2 celery sticks, 1 carrot – about 150 g (5 oz), 100 g (3½ oz) broccoli and 1 apple – about 100 g (3½ oz).

red refresher juice

Makes **about 300 ml**
   (½ pint)

2 **red peppers**, about 350 g
   (11½ oz) in total
1 **lime**, plus extra to decorate
½ **cucumber**, about 175 g
   (6 oz)
100 g (3½ oz) **broccoli**
ice cubes

Core and deseed the peppers. Roughly peel the lime. Juice together with the cucumber and broccoli.

Pour the juice into a glass over ice, add slices of lime and serve immediately.

For red hot juice, core and deseed 2 red peppers – about 350 g (11½ oz) in total. Juice the peppers with 1 small red chilli, 2 carrots – about 300 g (10 oz) in total – and 100 g (3½ oz) broccoli.

green goddess juice

Makes **about 300 ml**
  (½ pint)

150 g (5 oz) **broccoli**
2 **celery sticks**
2 **apples**, about 200 g (7 oz)
10 g (¹/₃ oz) **coriander leaves**
1–2 teaspoons **avocado oil**

Juice the broccoli with the celery, apple and coriander. Stir in the avocado oil.

Pour the juice into a glass and serve immediately.

For green refresher juice, juice 150 g (5 oz) broccoli with 2 celery sticks, 200 g (7 oz) peeled watermelon and ½ cucumber – about 175 g (6 oz). Serve poured over ice.

summer salad juice

Makes **about 300 ml**
   (½ pint)

1 **celery stick**
¼ **cucumber**, about 65 g
   (2½ oz)
2 **tomatoes**, about 200 g
   (7 oz) in total
2 **Little Gem lettuces**, about
   275g (9 oz) in total
2 **carrots**, about 300 g
   (10 oz) in total
1 **apple**, about 100 g (3½ oz)
ice cubes

Juice together the celery, cucumber, tomatoes, lettuce, carrots and apple.

Pour the juice into a glass over ice and serve immediately.

For minted summer salad juice, juice 1 cos lettuce – about 200 g (7 oz) – with ½ cucumber – about 175 g (6 oz), 2 carrots – about 300 g (10 oz) in total, 1 apple – about 100 g (3½ oz) – and a large bunch of mint. Serve poured over ice.

pepper punch

Makes **about 400 ml (14 fl oz)**

1 **red pepper**, about 175 g (6 oz)
1 **beetroot**, about 125 g (4 oz)
2 **carrots**, about 300 g (10 oz) in total
½ **lemon**
50 g (2 oz) **watercress**
ice cubes
pepper, to sprinkle

Core and deseed the red pepper. Juice together with the beetroot, carrots, lemon and watercress.

Pour the juice into a glass over ice, sprinkle with black pepper and serve immediately.

For hot pepper punch, core and deseed 1 red pepper – about 175 g (6 oz). Juice the pepper with 2 celery sticks, 3 tomatoes – about 300 g (10 oz) in total, 2 carrots – about 300 g (10 oz) in total – and a 2 cm (¾ inch) piece fresh horseradish root.

carrot, chilli & pineapple juice

Makes about **200 ml (7 fl oz)**

½ small **chilli**
250 g (8 oz) **pineapple**
250 g (8 oz) **carrot**
ice cubes
juice of ½ **lime**
1 tablespoon chopped **coriander leaves**

Deseed the chilli. Remove the core and peel from the pineapple. Juice the carrots with the chilli and pineapple.

Pour the juice into a glass over ice. Squeeze over the lime juice, stir in the chopped coriander and serve immediately.

For tomato, celery & ginger juice, trim 100 g (3½ oz) celery and peel and roughly chop 2.5 cm (1 inch) piece each of fresh root ginger and fresh horseradish root. Juice the celery, ginger and horseradish with 300 g (10 oz) tomatoes, 175 g (6 oz) carrot and a garlic clove. Serve over ice, decorated with celery slivers, if liked.

broccoli, spinach & apple juice

Makes **about 200 ml
(7 fl oz)**

150 g (5 oz) **broccoli**
150 g (5 oz) **spinach**
2 **apples**, about 200 g (7 oz)
2–3 **ice cubes**

Trim the broccoli. Juice the apples with the spinach and broccoli, alternating the spinach leaves with the other ingredients so that the spinach leaves do not clog the machine.

Transfer the juice to a food processor or blender, add a couple of ice cubes and process briefly.

Pour into a glass and serve immediately.

For spinach, apple & pepper juice, increase the apple to 250 g (8 oz) and, instead of broccoli, juice 100 g (3½ oz) yellow pepper. Stir in a pinch of ground cinnamon before serving.

fennel & camomile juice

Makes about **200 ml
(7 fl oz)**

1 **lemon**, plus extra to
   decorate
150 g (5 oz) **fennel bulb**
100 ml (3½ fl oz) chilled
   camomile tea
ice cubes

Roughly peel the lemon and juice it with the fennel.
Mix the juice with the chilled camomile tea.

Pour the combined juice and tea into a glass over ice
and serve with slices of lemon, to decorate.

For fennel & lettuce juice, juice 125 g (4 oz) fennel
bulb and 175 g (6 oz) lettuce with ½ lemon. Pour into
a glass over ice and decorate with a slice of lemon.

citrus detox juice

Makes **about 300 ml**
   (½ pint)

1 **beetroot**, about 175 g
   (6 oz)
1 **orange**, about 200 g (7 oz),
   roughly peeled
175 g (6 oz) **spring cabbage**

Juice all the ingredients together.

Pour the juice into a glass and serve immediately.

For daily detox juice, juice 1 lemon with 1 orange – about 200 g (7 oz) – and 175 g (6 oz) cabbage. Stir in 1 teaspoon ground linseeds and serve.

energy lift juice

Makes **about 350 ml (12 fl oz)**

1 large **carrot**, about 175 g (6 oz)
2 **celery sticks**
1 **sweet potato**, about 200 g (7 oz)
60 g (2¼ oz) **spinach**

Juice all the ingredients together.

Pour the juice into a glass and serve immediately.

For fennel energy lift juice, replace the celery with 1 fennel bulb – about 200 g (7 oz) – and juice as above. Serve sprinkled with a few fennel seeds.

fruit juices

pear & cranberry juice

Makes about **200 ml**
 (7 fl oz)

1 large **pear,** about 175 g
 (6 oz)
100 ml (3½ fl oz) **cranberry
 juice**
ice cubes

Juice the pear. Mix the pear juice with the cranberry juice.

Pour the combined juices into a glass over ice and serve immediately.

For cranberry & cucumber juice, use the same amount of cranberry juice and add the juice of 1 orange and 50 g (2 oz) cucumber.

green lemonade

Makes **about 500 ml
(17 fl oz)**

2 **lemons**, plus extra to
  decorate
30 g (1 ¼ oz) **spinach**
1 **cucumber**, about 350 g
  (11 ½ oz)
sparkling water

Juice the lemons with the spinach and cucumber.

Pour the juice into a glass, top up with sparkling
water and decorate with a wedge of lemon.

For citrusade, replace the spinach with 2 oranges
– about 325 g (11 oz) in total – and juice as above.

great grapefruit juice

Makes **about 350 ml (12 fl oz)**

2 **grapefruit**, about 300 g (10 oz)
1 **kiwifruit**, about 75 g (3 oz)
1 **apple**, about 100 g (3½ oz), plus extra to decorate
½ **cucumber**, about 175 g (6 oz)

Roughly peel the grapefruit and kiwifruit. Juice all the ingredients together.

Pour the juice into a glass, decorate with a slice of apple and serve immediately.

For hot & spicy grapefruit juice, add a 2 cm (¾ inch) piece of peeled fresh root ginger to the other ingredients and juice as above.

orange & raspberry juice

Makes about **500 ml (17 fl oz)**

2 large **oranges**, about 400 g (13 oz) in total
175 g (6 oz) **raspberries**
250 ml (8 fl oz) **water**
ice cubes (optional)

Roughly peel the oranges. Juice the oranges with the raspberries then add the water.

Pour the juice into 2 tall glasses over ice, if using, and serve immediately.

For orange & apricot juice, juice 300 g (10 oz) fresh, stoned apricots with 1 large orange – about 200 g (7 oz). Pour into tall glasses and top up with water to taste.

bouncing blueberry juice

Makes **about 300 ml**
  (½ pint)

300 g (10 oz) **blueberries**
½ **cucumber**, about 175 g
  (6 oz)
1 **apple**, about 100 g (3½ oz)

Juice all the ingredients together.

Pour the juice into a glass and serve immediately.

For blueberry power juice, add 200 g (7 oz) red cabbage to the other ingredients and juice as above.

exotic elixir

Makes **about 300 ml**
   (½ pint)

1 **orange**, about 200 g
   (6½ oz)
1 **kiwifruit**, about 75 g (3 oz),
   plus extra to decorate
2 **apricots**, about 125 g (4 oz)
   in total
1 slice **pineapple**, about
   180 g (6¼ oz)
1 large **carrot**, about
   160 g (5½ oz)

Roughly peel the orange and kiwifruit. Remove the stones from the apricots. Remove the skin from the pineapple. Juice all the ingredients together.

Pour the juice into a glass, decorate with a slice of kiwifruit and serve immediately.

For exotic sparkling juice, juice the ingredients as above. Pour the juice into a tall glass over ice and serve topped up with sparkling water.

cool currants juice

Makes **about 300 ml**
  (½ pint)

2 **apples**, about 200 g
  (7 oz) in total
300 g (10 oz) **blackcurrants**
100 g (3½ oz) **redcurrants**
sprig of **blackcurrants** or
  redcurrants, to decorate

Juice all the ingredients together.

Pour the juice into a glass, decorate with a sprig of currants and serve immediately.

For currant & berry juice, replace 100 g (3½ oz) of the blackcurrants with 100 g (3½ oz) mixed strawberries and blackberries and juice as above.

kiwi sparkler

Makes **about 300 ml**
   (½ pint)

3 **kiwifruit**, about 225 g
   (7½ oz) in total
2 cm (¾ inch) piece fresh
   root ginger
1 **apple**, about 100 g (3½ oz)
ice cubes (optional)
300 ml (½ pint) **sparkling**
   water

Peel the kiwifruit and ginger. Juice the kiwifruit with the ginger and apple.

Pour the juice into a tall glass over ice, if desired, top up with sparkling water and serve immediately.

For apple & pear sparkler, juice 2 apples – about 200 g (7 oz) in total, with 2 pears – about 300 g (10 oz) in total – and a 2 cm (¾ inch) piece fresh root ginger. Pour into a tall glass and top up with sparkling water.

five fruits juice

Makes **about 300 ml**
  (½ pint)

2 **clementines**, about 200 g
  (7 oz) in total
6 **cherries**
1 **apricot**, about 60 g (2¼ oz)
1 **apple**, about 100 g (3½ oz)
6 **red grapes**
1 **lemon grass** stalk
ice cubes

Peel the clementines. Stone the cherries and apricot. Juice together with the apple, grapes and lemon grass.

Pour the juice into a glass over ice and serve immediately.

For five citrus juice, roughly peel and juice 1 clementine – about 100 g (3½ oz) – with 1 grapefruit – about 275 g (9 oz), 1 orange – about 200 g (7 oz), 1 lemon and 1 lime. Serve poured over ice.

gingered pear juice

Makes **about 300 ml**
  (½ pint)

2 cm (¾ inch) piece fresh
  root ginger
5 **pears**, about 750 g (1 ½ lb)
  in total
large pinch of ground
  cinnamon
ice cubes

Peel the ginger. Juice the ginger with the pears. Stir in the cinnamon.

Pour the juice into a glass over ice and serve immediately.

For gingered mango juice, peel a 2 cm (¾ inch) piece fresh root ginger. Peel and stone 2 mangoes – about 400 g (13 oz) in total. Juice the ginger and mangoes with 2 apples – about 200 g (7 oz) in total. Serve poured over ice.

super fruits juice

Makes **about 300 ml (½ pint)**

1 **kiwifruit**, about 75 g (3 oz)
25 g (1 oz) fresh or frozen (defrosted) **cranberries**
50 g (2 oz) **pomegranate seeds**
100 g (3½ oz) **blueberries**
1 **carrot**, about 150 g (5 oz)

Peel the kiwifruit. Juice all the ingredients together.

Pour the juice into a glass and serve immediately.

For super spicy juice, juice 25 g (1 oz) fresh or frozen (defrosted) cranberries with 50 g (2 oz) pomegranate seeds, 2 cm (¾ inch) piece fresh root ginger, 1 apple – about 100 g (3½ oz) – and 100 g (3½ oz) raspberries. Stir in a large pinch of grated nutmeg before serving.

bitter berries juice

Makes **about 300 ml
(½ pint)**

100 g (3½ oz) **green cabbage**
12 **strawberries**, plus extra
to decorate
100 g (3½ oz) **blueberries**
100 g (3½ oz) **raspberries**
8 **grapes**

Juice all the ingredients together.

Pour the juice into a glass, decorate with extra strawberries and serve immediately.

For sweet berries juice, juice 100 g (3½ oz) each of strawberries, blackberries, raspberries and blueberries with 1 large carrot – about 175 g (6 oz) – and a small handful of mint.

minty apple tea

Makes **about 500 ml (17 fl oz)**

3 **apples**, about 300 g (10 oz) in total
large handful **mint**, plus extra sprigs to decorate
200 ml (7 fl oz) chilled **mint tea**
ice cubes

Juice the apples and mint. Stir in the chilled mint tea.

Pour the combined juice and tea into a glass over ice, decorate with a sprig of mint and serve.

For cinnamon apple tea, juice 4 apples – about 400 g (13 oz) in total. Stir in 200 ml (7 fl oz) chilled tea, add a large pinch of ground cinnamon and stir to combine. Serve poured over crushed ice with a cinnamon stick for stirring.

forest fruits juice

Makes **about 300 ml**
  (½ pint)

200 g (7 oz) **blackberries**
100 g (3½ oz) **blueberries**
1 **apple**, about 100 g (3½ oz)

Juice all the ingredients together.

Pour the juice into a glass and serve immediately.

For green forest fruits juice, juice 1 apple – about 100 g (3½ oz) – with 200 g (7 oz) blackberries, 30 g (1¼ oz) kale and a 2 cm (¾ inch) piece peeled fresh root ginger.

mango, melon & orange juice

Makes **about 400 ml**
  (14 fl oz)

2 **oranges**, about 400 g
  (13 oz)
1 ripe **mango**, about 200 g
  (7 oz)
½ **Galia melon**, about
  200 g (7 oz)
2 **ice cubes**

Roughly peel and juice the oranges.

Stone and peel the mango. Peel the melon as close to the skin as possible.

Place the mango and melon in a food processor or blender and process until smooth. Add the orange juice and ice cubes, then process until smooth.

Pour the juice into a glass and serve immediately.

For coconut & pineapple juice, place 1 x 400 g (13 oz) can coconut milk in a food processor or blender with ½ small pineapple, peeled, cored and roughly chopped. Process until smooth, then serve poured over ice and decorated with cherries or strawberries.

citrus green juice

Makes **about 350 ml
  (12 fl oz)**

1 **lime**
1 **orange**, about 200 g (7 oz)
1 **grapefruit**, about 275 g
  (9 oz)
1 teaspoon **agave syrup**
½ tablespoon **wheatgrass
  powder**

Roughly peel the lime, orange and grapefruit. Juice all the fruits together. Stir in the agave syrup and wheatgrass powder.

Pour the juice into a glass and serve immediately.

For gingered green juice, juice 2 oranges – about 400 g (13 oz) in total, with 2 carrots – about 300 g (10 oz) in total, 1 apple – about 100 g (3½ oz) – and a 2 cm (¾ inch) piece peeled fresh root ginger. Stir in ½ tablespoon barleygrass or wheatgrass powder and serve.

blackberry, melon & kiwifruit juice

Makes about **250 ml**
  (8 fl oz)

100 g (3½ oz) **cantaloupe melon**
2 **kiwifruit**, about 150 g (5 oz)
100 g (3½ oz) fresh or frozen **blackberries**, plus extra to decorate
2–3 **ice cubes**

Peel the melon as close to the skin as possible. Roughly peel the kiwifruit. Juice the melon with the kiwifruit and blackberries.

Transfer the juice to a food processor or blender and process with a couple of ice cubes.

Pour into a glass and decorate with a few blackberries.

For melon & cherry juice, peel and roughly chop 300 g (10 oz) honeydew melon. Juice the melon flesh with 125 g (4 oz) stoned cherries and serve.

crazy cranberry juice

Makes **about 350ml**
 (12 fl oz)

1 **orange**, about 200 g
 (7 oz)
225 g (7½ oz) **cranberries**
2 **carrots**, about 300g
 (10 oz) in total

Roughly peel the orange. Juice the orange with the cranberries and carrots.

Pour the juice into a glass and serve immediately.

For cranberry fizz, juice 225 g (7½ oz) cranberries with 100 g (3½ oz) raspberries and 1 apple – about 100 g (3½ oz). Serve poured over ice and topped up with sparkling water.

pineapple, grape & celery juice

Makes **about 200 ml**
  (7 fl oz)

125 g (4 oz) **pineapple**
125 g (4 oz) **green grapes**
50 g (2 oz) **celery**
50 g (2 oz) **lettuce**
2–3 **ice cubes** (optional)

Remove the skin and core from the pineapple. Juice the pineapple with the grapes, celery and lettuce.

Pour the juice into a glass over ice, if using, and serve immediately.

For pineapple & pear juice, double the amount of pineapple and replace the grapes, celery and lettuce with 2 pears – about 350 g (11½ oz) in total – and ½ a lime.

thick & creamy raspberry juice

Makes **about 200 ml
(7 fl oz)**

1 **apricot**, about 60 g (2¼ oz)
200 g (7 oz) **raspberries**,
   plus extra to decorate
12 **red grapes**
1 **carrot**, about 150 g (5 oz)

Stone the apricot. Juice all the ingredients together.

Pour the juice into a glass, decorate with a few raspberries and serve immediately.

For thick & creamy mango juice, stone 2 apricots – about 125 g (4 oz) in total. Peel and stone 1 mango – about 200 g (7 oz). Juice the apricots and mango with 12 green grapes and 1 carrot – about 150 g (5 oz) – and serve.

apple, cranberry & blueberry juice

Makes **about 300 ml
(10 fl oz)**

3 **apples**, about 300 g
(10 oz) in total
150 ml (5 fl oz) **unsweetened
cranberry juice**
125 g (4 oz) fresh or frozen
blueberries
1 tablespoon **powdered
psyllium husks** (optional)
ice cubes (optional)

Juice the apples.

Transfer the apple juice to a food processor or blender,
add the cranberry juice, blueberries and powdered
psyllium husks, if using, and process until smooth.

Pour the juice into a glass over ice, if using, and serve
immediately.

For cranberry, apple & lettuce juice, juice ½ an apple
– about 50 g (2 oz) – and 125 g (4 oz) lettuce with
50 g (2 oz) cranberries. Serve over ice.

peachy plum juice

Makes **about 300 ml**
  (½ pint)

4 **plums**, about 300 g (10 oz)
  in total
3 **peaches**, about 450 g
  (14½ oz) in total
2 **apricots**, about 150 g (5 oz)
  in total
1 **carrot**, about 150 g (5 oz)
ice cubes

Remove the stones from the plums, peaches and apricots. Juice all the ingredients together.

Pour the juice into a glass over ice and serve immediately.

For gingered plum juice, stone 4 plums – about 300 g (10 oz) in total. Juice the plums with 2 carrots – about 300 g (10 oz) in total – and a 2 cm (¾ inch) piece peeled fresh root ginger. Stir in a large pinch of grated nutmeg and serve.

pomegranate plus juice

Makes **about 250 ml
(8 fl oz)**

1 **lemon**
2 **pomegranates**, about
500 g (1 lb) in total
200 g (7 oz) **blueberries**

Roughly peel the lemon. Remove the seeds from the pomegranate by cutting the fruit in half, then holding the halved fruit over a bowl and hitting the skin with a wooden spoon so that the seeds fall into the bowl. Juice all the ingredients together.

Pour the juice into a glass and serve immediately.

For peachy pomegranate juice, remove the seeds from 1 pomegranate – about 250 g (8 oz) in total. Juice the pomegranate seeds with 2 stoned peaches – about 300 g (10 oz) in total, 1 apple – about 100 g (3½ oz) – and 1 carrot – about 150 g (5 oz).

virgin pina colada juice

Makes **about 400 ml (14 fl oz)**

400 g (13 oz) **pineapple**, plus a small pineapple wedge to decorate
200 ml (7 fl oz) **coconut water**
ice cubes

Peel and juice the pineapple. Stir the coconut water into the pineapple juice.

Pour the combined juice and coconut water into a glass over ice, decorate with a wedge of pineapple and serve immediately.

For mango & coconut juice, juice 3 peeled and stoned mangoes – about 600 g (1 lb 3½ oz) in total. Stir in 200 ml (7 fl oz) coconut water and serve poured over ice with a slice of mango to decorate.

blackberry, apple & celeriac juice

Makes about **200 ml**
(7 fl oz)

100 g (3½ oz) **celeriac**
50 g (2 oz) **apple**
100 g (3½ oz) frozen
 blackberries, plus extra
 to decorate
2–3 **ice cubes**

Peel the celeriac. Juice the celeriac with the apple.

Transfer the juice to a food processor or blender, add
the blackberries and the ice cubes and process briefly.

Pour the juice into a glass, decorate with extra
blackberries and serve immediately.

For blackberry & pineapple juice, juice 150 g (5 oz)
each of blackberries and pineapple with 25 g (1 oz)
apple. Serve in a tall glass over ice.

watermelon & raspberry juice

Makes **about 200 ml**
  (7 fl oz)

300 g (10 oz) **watermelon**
125 g (4 oz) **raspberries**
crushed ice (optional)

Peel the melon as close to the skin as possible and roughly chop.

Transfer the watermelon and raspberries to a food processor or blender and process until smooth.

Press the juice through a sieve over a bowl to remove any raspberry pips.

Pour the juice into glasses over some crushed ice, if liked.

For melon & apple juice, place 200 g (7 oz) peeled and chopped green melon into a food processor or blender with 1 green apple – about 100 g (3½ oz) – cored and cut into wedges. Add 1 tablespoon lemon juice and process until smooth. Pour over crushed ice, if liked.

pear, kiwifruit & lime juice

Makes **about 300 ml**
  (½ pint)

3 **kiwifruit**, about 225 g
  (7½ oz) in total, plus extra
  to decorate
2 **pears**, about 350 g
  (11½ oz) in total
½ **lime**
2–3 **ice cubes** (optional)

Peel the kiwifruit. Juice the kiwifruit with the pears and lime.

Pour into a tall glass, add the ice cubes, if using, decorate with slices of kiwifruit and serve immediately.

For grape & kiwifruit juice, replace the pears and lime with 300 g (10 oz) green grapes.

spiced melon juice

Makes **about 450 ml (¾ pint)**

250 g (8 oz) **cantaloupe melon**
500 g (1 lb) **watermelon**
50 g (2 oz) **spinach**
2 cm (¾ inch) piece fresh **root ginger**
2–3 **ice cubes**
grated **nutmeg**, to sprinkle

Peel both melons as close to the skin as possible. Juice the melons with the spinach and ginger.

Transfer the juice to a food processor or blender, add a handful of ice cubes and process for 10 seconds.

Serve in a glass, sprinkled with nutmeg.

For spicy melon & carrot juice, replace the spinach with 1 large carrot – about 160 g (5½ oz) – and juice as above.

juicy
smoothies

banana & maple syrup smoothie

Serves **2**

2 **bananas**
300 ml (½ pint) **milk**
4 tablespoons **natural
 fromage frais**
3 tablespoons **maple syrup**
50 g (2 oz) hot **oat cereal**

To decorate
banana slices
malt loaf chunks

Peel and chop the bananas.

Place the bananas in a food processor or blender with the milk, fromage frais and maple syrup and process until smooth. Add the oat cereal and process again to thicken.

Pour into 2 glasses. Arrange banana slices and chunks of malt loaf on 2 cocktail sticks and balance them across the top of the glasses, to decorate.

For peanut butter smoothies, replace the bananas with 4 tablespoons crunchy peanut butter, and change the maple syrup to honey. Make as above, processing until smooth.

breakfast smoothie

Serves **2**

2 **oranges**, about 400 g
  (13 oz)
1 **banana**
2 tablespoons **muesli**
300 ml (½ pint) **milk**
ground **cinnamon**, to sprinkle

Roughly peel and juice the oranges. Peel the banana.

Transfer the orange juice and banana to a food processor or blender, add the muesli and milk and process until smooth.

Pour the smoothie into 2 glasses, sprinkle with ground cinnamon and serve immediately.

For nutty breakfast smoothie, follow the recipe above, replacing 1 tablespoon muesli with 1 tablespoon nuts of your choice (walnuts and pecans both work really well).

shocking pink smoothie

Serves **2**

1 **beetroot**, about 125 g (4 oz)
1 **banana**
85 g (3¼ oz) **strawberries**, plus extra to decorate
60 g (2¼ oz) **raspberries**
1 tablespoon **flaked almonds**
300 ml (½ pint) **milk**
ice cubes

Juice the beetroot. Peel the banana.

Transfer the beetroot juice and banana to a food processor or blender, add the berries, almonds and milk and process until smooth.

Pour the smoothie into 2 tall glasses over ice, decorate with strawberries and serve immediately.

For shocking pink protein boost, follow the recipe above, adding 2 tablespoons whey protein powder to the food processor or blender with the other ingredients. If the smoothie is a little too thick, just add another dash of milk.

digestive delight smoothie

Serves **2**

1 **papaya**, about 250 g (8 oz)
1 **apricot**, about 75 g (3 oz)
1 **lime**, plus extra to decorate
400 ml (14 fl oz) **hemp milk**
1 teaspoon **chia oil**
¼ teaspoon ground **cinnamon**

Peel and deseed the papaya. Stone the apricot. Roughly peel and then juice the lime.

Transfer the papaya, apricot and lime juice to a food processor or blender, add the remaining ingredients and process until smooth.

Pour the smoothie into 2 glasses, add a wedge of lime to each glass and serve immediately.

For minty digestive delight smoothie, follow the recipe above, adding 10–12 mint leaves to the food processor or blender with the other ingredients.

strawberries & custard smoothie

Serves **1**

1 **orange**, about 200 g (7 oz)
1 **mango**, about 200 g (7 oz)
100 ml (3½ fl oz) **milk**
60 g (2¼ oz) **strawberries**

Roughly peel and then juice the orange. Stone and peel the mango.

Transfer the orange juice and mango to a food processor or blender, add the milk and process until smooth. Pour the mixture into a glass.

Put the strawberries in the food processor or blender with 1 tablespoon of water and process until smooth.

Pour the strawberry mixture into the glass on top of the mango mixture. Stir a little to create swirls of the strawberry mixture in the smoothie.

For raspberries & custard smoothie, follow the recipe above, replacing the strawberries with 100 g (3½ oz) raspberries.

perfect passion smoothie

Serves **4**

1 **lime**
2 large **mangoes**, about
   1.15 kg (2¼ lb)
5 **passionfruit**
225 g (7½ oz) **natural yogurt**
2 handfuls **ice cubes**

Roughly peel and then juice the lime. Peel and stone the mangoes.

Transfer the lime juice and mangoes to a food processor or blender. Halve the passionfruit, scoop out the pulp and add all but 1 tablespoon to the blender with the yogurt and ice cubes and process until smooth.

Pour the smoothie into 4 glasses, decorate with the remaining passionfruit pulp and serve immediately.

For passionfruit & banana smoothie, juice 1 roughly peeled lime. Transfer the juice to a food processor or blender, add 2 peeled bananas, the pulp of 4 passionfruit and 600 ml (1 pint) milk and process until smooth.

nectarine & raspberry yogurt ice

Serves **2**

3 **nectarines**, about
   450 g (14½ oz)
175 g (6 oz) **raspberries**
150 ml (¼ pint) **natural yogurt**
handful of **ice cubes**

Halve and stone the nectarines.

Put the nectarines and raspberries in a food processor or blender and process until really smooth. Add the yogurt and process again, then add the ice and process until very crushed and the shake thickens.

Pour into 2 chilled glasses. Decorate with cocktail umbrellas and anything else to make the drink look fun!

For banana & mango coconut ice, replace the nectarines and raspberries with 1 large banana and 1 mango – about 200 g (7 oz) – cut into chunks and process until smooth. Add 150 ml (¼ pint) coconut milk and process again. Add the ice and process until the shake thickens. Pour into chilled glasses to serve.

probiotic smoothie

Serves **1**

1 **orange**, about 200 g (7 oz)
1 **mango**, about 200 g (7 oz)
200 g (7 oz) **kefir**
150 g (5 oz) **blueberries**

Roughly peel and then juice the orange. Peel and stone the mango.

Transfer the orange juice and mango to a food processor or blender, add the kefir and blueberries and process until smooth.

Pour the smoothie into a glass and serve immediately.

For kefir & berry smoothie, juice 1 roughly peeled orange – about 200 g (7 oz). Transfer the juice to a food processor or blender, add 200 g (7 oz) kefir and 150 g (5 oz) frozen mixed berries and process until smooth.

energizer smoothie

Serves **2**

1 **beetroot**, about 200 g
  (7 oz)
6 stoned **dates**
1 tablespoon **rolled oats**
100 g (3½ oz) **blackberries**
1 teaspoon **maca powder**
500 ml (17 fl oz) **almond milk**
1 teaspoon **ground flaxseed**
ice cubes

Juice the beetroot.

Transfer the juice to a food processor or blender, add the remaining ingredients (except the ice cubes) and process until smooth.

Pour the smoothie into 2 glasses over ice and serve immediately.

For spicy energizer smoothie, juice 1 beetroot – about 200 g (7 oz) – with a 3 cm (1¼ inch) piece peeled fresh root ginger and 1 lemon grass stalk. Transfer the juice to a blender or food processor, add 6 figs, 1 tablespoon rolled oats, 100 g (3½ oz) strawberries, 1 teaspoon maca powder and 500 ml (17 fl oz) almond milk and process until smooth.

superfood smoothie

Serves **2**

25 g (1 oz) **cranberries**
50 g (2 oz) **pomegranate seeds**
25 g (1 oz) **kale**
1 **beetroot**, about 100 g (3½ oz)
1 **banana**
1 tablespoon **goji berries**
50 g (2 oz) **strawberries**
500 ml (17 fl oz) **hemp milk**
1 tablespoon **avocado oil**
1 tablespoon **toasted sesame seeds**, to sprinkle

Juice the cranberries with the pomegranate seeds, kale and beetroot.

Transfer the juice to a food processor or blender, add the remaining ingredients and process until smooth.

Pour the smoothie into 2 glasses, sprinkle with toasted sesame seeds and serve immediately.

For superfood green smoothie, juice 50 g (2 oz) kale with 2 celery sticks and a 2 cm (¾ inch) piece peeled fresh root ginger. Transfer the juice to a food processor or blender, add 1 peeled and stoned avocado, 1 peeled garlic clove, 1 cucumber – about 350 g (11½ oz), 15 g (½ oz) parsley, salt and pepper and a large handful of ice cubes and process until smooth.

berry blast smoothie

Serves **2**

2 **apples**, about 200 g
 (7 oz)
1 large **banana**
250 g (8 oz) **mixed berries**
 (such as blueberries,
 blackberries, raspberries
 and strawberries), plus
 extra to decorate
ice cubes

Juice the apples. Peel the banana.

Transfer the apple juice and banana to a food processor or blender, add the mixed berries and process until smooth, adding a little water, if necessary, if you want a looser consistency.

Pour the smoothie into 2 glasses over ice, decorate with a few extra berries and serve immediately.

For berry green smoothie, follow the recipe above, adding 60 g (2¼ oz) spinach to the juicer with the apple.

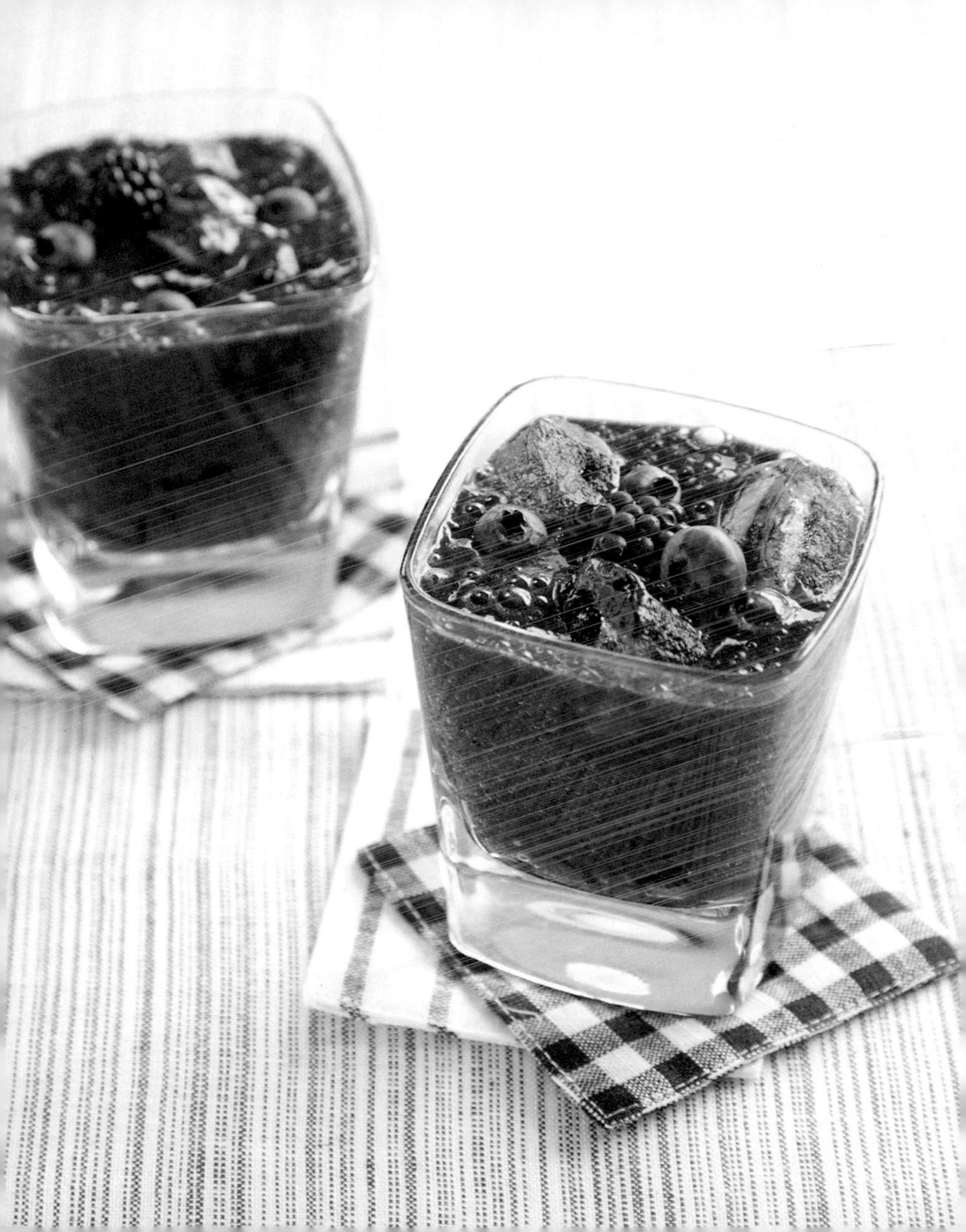

cherry & chocolate smoothie

Serves **2**

100 g (3½ oz) **blueberries**
200 g (7 oz) **cherries**
1 tablespoon **cocoa nibs,** plus
    extra to sprinkle
300 ml (½ pint) **milk**

Juice the blueberries. Stone the cherries.

Transfer the blueberry juice and cherries to a food processor or blender, add the cocoa nibs and milk and process until smooth.

Pour the smoothie into 2 glasses, sprinkle with some extra cocoa nibs and serve immediately.

For breakfast cherry & chocolate smoothie, follow the recipe above, adding 1 tablespoon cashew nuts and 1 tablespoon rolled oats to the food processor or blender with the other ingredients.

peanut butter & banana smoothie

Serves **4**

½ **lime**
150g (5 oz) **banana**
1 tablespoon **peanut butter**
300 ml (½ pint) **almond milk**
grated **nutmeg**, to sprinkle

Roughly peel and then juice the lime. Peel the banana.

Transfer the lime juice and banana to a food processor or blender, add the peanut butter and almond milk and process until smooth.

Pour the smoothie into 4 glasses, sprinkle with a large pinch of nutmeg and serve immediately.

For peanut butter & blueberry smoothie, roughly peel and juice ½ lime. Transfer the juice to a food processor or blender, add 100 g (3½ oz) blueberries, 1 tablespoon peanut butter and 300 ml (½ pint) milk and process until smooth.

fruity summer shake

Serves **4**

2 **peaches**, about
  300 g (10 oz)
300 g (10 oz) **strawberries**
300 g (10 oz) **raspberries**
400 ml (14 fl oz) **milk**
ice cubes

Halve and stone the peaches.

Put the peaches in a food processor or blender with the strawberries and raspberries and process to a smooth purée. Add the milk and blend the ingredients again until the mixture is smooth and frothy.

Pour the shake into 4 tall glasses over the ice cubes.

For soya milk & mango shake, replace the peach, strawberries and raspberries with 2 large mangoes – about 400 g (13 oz) – peeled and stoned, and the juice of 2 oranges. Purée as above, then pour in 400 ml (14 fl oz) soya milk, blend and serve over ice cubes as above.

bursting baobab smoothie

Serves **4**

1 **orange**, about 160 g
  (5½ oz)
1 **mango**, about 200 g (7 oz)
1 small **banana**
3 **ice cubes**
1 tablespoon **baobab powder**
300 ml (½ pint) **water**

Roughly peel and then juice the orange. Peel and stone the mango. Peel the banana.

Transfer the orange juice to a food processor or blender, add the mango, banana and the remaining ingredients and process until smooth.

Pour the smoothie into glasses and serve immediately.

For bursting blueberry smoothie, juice 1 small beetroot – about 100g (3½ oz). Transfer the juice to a food processor or blender, add 1 small peeled banana, 200 g (7 oz) blueberries, 3 ice cubes, 1 tablespoon baobab powder and 300 ml (½ pint) water and process until smooth.

extra-thick berry smoothie

Serves **4**

3 tablespoons **crème de cassis** or **spiced red fruit cordial**

250 g (8 oz) **mixed frozen berries**

500 g (1 lb) fat-free **fromage frais**

400 ml (14 fl oz) **milk**

1 **vanilla pod**, split in half lengthways

toasted flaked almonds, to decorate

Put the crème de cassis or cordial in a saucepan over a low heat and gently heat, then add the berries. Stir, cover and cook for about 5 minutes or until the fruit has thawed and is beginning to collapse. Remove from the heat and cool completely.

Process most of the berry mixture with the fromage frais and milk in a food processor or blender until smooth.

Scrape in the seeds from the vanilla pod and beat to combine.

Fold the reserved berries into the fromage frais mixture until just combined. Spoon into 4 glasses and serve immediately, decorated with toasted almonds.

For extra-thick exotic fruit smoothie, replace the crème de cassis with 3 tablespoons coconut cream and the mixed berries with 250 g (8 oz) exotic fruit mix and add 1 tablespoon lime juice. Heat as above, then blend in a food processor or blender until smooth. Chill as above. Mix the fromage frais with 2 tablespoons coconut cream and 250 g (8 oz) fat-free mango yogurt instead of the milk. Fold in the fruit purée and serve sprinkled with toasted coconut flakes, if liked.

recovery smoothie

Serves **4**

2 **kiwifruit**, about 150 g (5 oz)

5 **dried figs**

300 ml (½ pint) **almond milk**

1 tablespoon **protein powder**

4 **walnut halves**

¼ teaspoon ground **cinnamon**

Peel and then juice the kiwifruit.

Transfer the juice to a food processor or blender, add the remaining ingredients and process until smooth.

Pour the smoothie into 4 glasses and serve immediately.

For nutty recovery smoothie, peel and juice 2 kiwifruit – about 150 g (5 oz). Transfer the juice to a food processor or blender, add 3 tablespoons peanut butter, 300 ml (½ pint) almond milk, 1 tablespoon cocoa nibs and 1 tablespoon protein powder and process until smooth.

creamy green smoothie

Serves **2**

1 **avocado**

1 **lime**

30 g (1 ¼ oz) **spinach**

2 **celery sticks**, plus extra
   to decorate

1 **garlic clove**

25 g (1 oz) **parsley**

1 teaspoon **green powder**
   (such as spirulina,
   wheatgrass or chlorella)

salt and **pepper**

Peel and stone the avocado. Roughly peel the lime. Juice the lime with the spinach.

Transfer the avocado and the juice to a food processor or blender, add the remaining ingredients and enough water to just cover, and process until smooth. Season the smoothie to taste with salt and pepper and process again.

Pour the smoothie into 2 glasses, add a trimmed celery stick to each glass and serve immediately.

For spicy green smoothie, follow the recipe above, adding a 2 cm (¾ inch) piece peeled fresh root ginger and ½ deseeded red chilli to the food processor or blender with the other ingredients.

melon, mint & berry smoothie

Serves **4**

1 kg (2 lb) **watermelon**
14–16 **strawberries**
12 **mint leaves**
small handful of **ice cubes**

Peel the melon as close to the skin as possible. Hull the strawberries.

Place all the ingredients in a food processor or blender and process until smooth.

Pour into 4 glasses and serve immediately.

For melon, mint and strawberry soup, place 200 g (7 oz) peeled, deseeded and chopped cantaloupe melon in a food processor or blender and process until smooth. Pour into a jug, cover and chill for 20 minutes. Clean the food processor or blender and repeat with 1 small peeled, deseeded and chopped honeydew melon and then 150 g (5 oz) hulled and chopped strawberries. When ready to serve, pour a ladle of each fruit purée into a bowl and make a pattern by dragging a knife through each one. Serve sprinkled with 2 tablespoons hulled and chopped strawberries and 2 teaspoons chopped mint.

summer smoothie

Serves **1**

½ **lime**
small handful **mint**, plus
   an extra sprig to decorate
125 g (4 oz) **gooseberries**
30 g (1¼ oz) **ground
   almonds**
150 ml (¼ pint) **non-dairy
   milk**
1 teaspoon **elderflower
   cordial**

Roughly peel the lime. Juice the lime with the mint.

Transfer the juice to a food processor or blender, add the remaining ingredients and process until smooth.

Pour the smoothie into a glass, decorate with a sprig of mint and serve immediately.

For strawberry summer smoothie, juice ½ roughly peeled lime and a small handful of mint. Transfer the juice to a food processor or blender, add 125g (4 oz) strawberries, 30 g (¼ oz) ground almonds and 150 ml (¼ pint) milk and process until smooth. Decorate with a sprig of mint.

mango & passion fruit smoothie

Serves **4**

1 large **mango**, about
   200 g (7 oz)
750 g (1 ½ lb) **natural yogurt**
1–2 tablespoons **agave
   nectar**, to taste
1 **vanilla pod**, split in half
   lengthways
4 **passionfruit**, halved

Stone and peel the mango.

Transfer the mango to a food processor or blender and process to a purée.

Put the yogurt and agave nectar, according to taste, in a large bowl, scrape in the seeds from the vanilla pod and beat together. Gently fold in the mango purée and spoon into tall glasses.

Scoop the seeds from the passion fruit and spoon over the smoothie. Serve immediately with thin biscuits, if liked.

For blackcurrant & almond smoothie, purée 250 g (8 oz) blackcurrants as above and fold into the yogurt with the agave nectar, according to taste, and 1 teaspoon almond essence. Spoon into tall glasses and decorate with toasted almonds, to serve.

blueberry & mint smoothie

Serves **2**

100 g (3½ oz) **frozen blueberries**
150 ml (¼ pint) **soya milk**
small bunch of **mint**

Put the blueberries in a food processor or blender and pour in the soya milk. Pull the mint leaves off their stalks, reserving one or two sprigs for decoration, and add the remainder to the blender. Process briefly.

Pour the smoothie into 2 glasses, decorate with the reserved mint sprigs and serve immediately.

For blueberry & apple smoothie, process 250 g (8 oz) apples with 125 g (4 oz) blueberries in a food processor or blender until smooth.

juicy dips

red pepper & spring onion dip

Serves **4**

1 large **red pepper**, cut
 into quarters, cored and
 deseeded
2 **garlic cloves,** unpeeled
250 g (8 oz) **natural yogurt**
2 **spring onions**, finely
 chopped
pepper
selection of **raw vegetables**,
 such as carrots, cucumber,
 peppers, fennel bulb,
 tomatoes, baby corn,
 mangetout, celery and
 courgettes, cut into batons,
 to serve

Slightly flatten the pepper quarters and place on a baking sheet. Wrap the garlic in foil and place on the sheet. Roast in a preheated oven, 220°C (425°F), Gas Mark 7, for 30–40 minutes until the pepper is slightly charred and the garlic is soft.

When cool enough to handle, remove the skin from the pepper and discard. Transfer the flesh to a food processor or blender. Squeeze in the roasted garlic flesh from the cloves and process until smooth.

Stir in the yogurt and spring onions. Season to taste with pepper and serve with the vegetable batons.

For aubergine & yogurt dip, roast a whole aubergine in a preheated oven, 220°C (425°F), Gas Mark 7, with the garlic for 30–40 minutes, omitting the red pepper. If the aubergine is still not tender after the cooking time, carefully turn it over and bake for a further 10–15 minutes until very soft. Cut the aubergine in half and scoop the flesh out into a food processor or blender. Squeeze in the roasted garlic flesh from the cloves, add a handful of basil leaves and season with salt and pepper. Process until smooth. Stir in the yogurt and spring onions. Serve with the vegetable batons.

spinach & bean dip

Serves **2**

50 g (2 oz) **baby spinach**
  leaves
1 **celery stick**
1 x 400 g (13 oz) can **white**
  kidney beans, drained
salt and **pepper**
vegetable crudités, to serve

Juice the spinach with the celery.

Pour the juice into a food processor or blender, add the kidney beans and process until smooth. Season to taste and serve with vegetable crudités.

For nutty bean dip, follow the recipe above, adding 50 g (2 oz) walnuts (or your favourite nuts) to the food processor or blender with the juice and kidney beans.

beetroot & orange hummus

Serves **4**

2 x 400 g (13 oz) cans
   chickpeas, drained
3 **garlic cloves,** peeled
1½ tablespoons **tahini**
1 **beetroot**
1 **orange**, roughly peeled
2–3 tablespoons **olive oil**
salt and **pepper**
oatcakes or **crispbreads**,
   to serve

Place the chickpeas and garlic cloves in a food processor or blender and process until broken down. Add the tahini and process for another 5–10 seconds.

Juice the beetroot with the orange. Pour the juice into the food processor or blender and process again, gradually adding the olive oil until you have the consistency you prefer. Season to taste and serve with oatcakes or crispbreads.

For herby hummus, follow the recipe above, omitting the beetroot and adding a small handful of coriander leaves to the food processor or blender with the chickpeas and garlic.

blue cheese & celery dip

Serves **2**

3 **celery sticks**
150 g (5 oz) **blue cheese**
vegetable crudités, to serve

Juice the celery.

Transfer the celery juice to a food processor or blender, add the cheese and process until smooth. Serve with vegetable crudités.

For cream cheese & pepper dip, juice 1 cored and deseeded red pepper. Pour the juice into a small bowl, add 200 g (7 oz) cream cheese (or more depending on your preferred thickness of dip) and stir to combine.

rocket & macadamia nut dip

Serves **2**

½ **celery stick**
30 g (1¼ oz) **spinach**
20 g (¾ oz) **rocket**
50 g (2 oz) **macadamia nuts**
½ **garlic clove**, peeled
1 tablespoon grated
  Parmesan
1–2 tablespoons **olive oil**
salt and **pepper**
toasted **pitta bread**, to serve

Juice the celery with the spinach.

Transfer the juice to a food processor or blender, add the rocket, macadamia nuts, garlic and Parmesan and process until smooth, gradually adding the olive oil until you have the consistency you prefer. Season to taste and serve with toasted pitta bread.

For watercress & walnut dip, follow the recipe above, replacing the rocket with 20 g (¾ oz) watercress and the macadamia nuts with 50 g (2 oz) walnuts.

tomato salsa

Serves **4**

4 large **tomatoes**
½ **lime**, roughly peeled
½ **red pepper**, cored and
  deseeded
1 **green chilli**, finely chopped
½ medium **red onion**, diced
20 g (¾ oz) **coriander leaves**,
  chopped
salt and **pepper**
tortilla chips, to serve

Score a cross into the base of each tomato with a sharp knife and place in a large bowl. Pour over boiling water to cover and leave for 20 seconds. Transfer the tomatoes to a bowl of iced water using a slotted spoon and allow to cool slightly. When cool, peel off the skins. Cut the tomatoes in half, remove and discard the seeds and chop the tomato flesh.

Juice the lime with the red pepper. Transfer the juice to a bowl.

Add the chopped tomatoes to the juice along with the chilli, red onion and coriander. Stir to combine and season to taste. Serve with tortilla chips.

For avocado & tomato salsa, follow the recipe above, replacing 2 of the tomatoes with 1 large avocado. Peel, stone and dice the avocado and stir into the salsa with the chilli, onion and coriander.

asparagus, feta & white bean dip

Serves **2**

125 g (4 oz) **asparagus spears**
1 x 400 g (13 oz) can **cannellini beans**, drained
1 **garlic clove**, peeled
50 g (2 oz) **feta cheese**
1 tablespoon **olive oil**
pepper
cooked king prawns, to serve

Juice the asparagus.

Transfer the juice to a food processor or blender, add the beans, garlic, feta and olive oil, and process until smooth. Season to taste and serve with king prawns for dipping.

For tomato & butterbean dip, juice 2 large tomatoes. Transfer the juice to a food processor or blender, add 1 x 400 g (13 oz) drained can butterbeans, 15 g (½ oz) parsley and 1 peeled garlic clove and process until smooth, gradually adding olive oil until you have the consistency you prefer. Season to taste and serve.

french onion dip

Serves **2**

½ tablespoon **olive oil**
4 **onions**, peeled and finely
chopped
1 **garlic clove**, crushed
½ tablespoon **Worcestershire
sauce**
leaves from 2 **thyme sprigs**
200 g (7 oz) **Greek yogurt**
2 cm (¾ inch) piece fresh
horseradish root, peeled
salt and **pepper**

Heat the oil in a frying pan. Add the onions and cook over a low heat for 18–20 minutes, stirring from time to time, until they start to caramelize and turn golden. Stir in the crushed garlic and cook for a further 2 minutes, then stir in the Worcestershire sauce and thyme leaves and remove from the heat. Leave to cool.

Transfer the onion mixture to a bowl and stir in the yogurt.

Juice the horseradish and add the juice to the onion dip. Season to taste and serve.

For celery & onion dip, follow the recipe above, replacing 2 of the onions with 3 finely sliced celery sticks and omitting the thyme leaves.

digestive dip

Serves **2**

1 **lime**
2 **papaya**, about 500 g (1 lb),
   peeled and deseeded
100 g (3½ oz) **natural yogurt**
fresh fruit, to serve

Grate the rind of the lime and reserve. Juice the lime.

Transfer the juice to a food processor or blender, add the papaya and yogurt and process until smooth. Stir in the reserved grated lime rind. Serve with fresh fruit for dipping.

For lime & apple dip, prepare the lime as above. Pour the lime juice into a bowl and add 200 g (7 oz) natural yogurt with 2 grated apples. Mix to combine. Stir in the grated lime zest and a large pinch of cinnamon. Serve with fresh fruit for dipping.

satay dip

Serves **2**

1 **lime**, roughly peeled
2 cm (¾ inch) piece fresh **root ginger**, peeled
1 **garlic clove**, peeled
3 tablespoons **smooth peanut butter**
3–4 tablespoons **coconut milk**
½ teaspoon **soy sauce**
1 tablespoon chopped **coriander leaves**
chicken kebabs, to serve

Juice the lime with the ginger.

Transfer the juice to a food processor or blender, add the garlic, peanut butter, coconut milk and soy sauce and process until combined. Stir in the chopped coriander. Serve with chicken kebabs.

For hot & crunchy satay dip, follow the recipe above, adding 1 red chilli to the blender with the other ingredients and stirring 1 tablespoon chopped hazelnuts into the dip with the chopped coriander.

carrot & cashew dip

Serves **4**

2 **oranges**, roughly peeled
2 **carrots**, peeled and
   thinly sliced
1 tablespoon **cashew nuts**
8 **dried apricots**, diced
1 teaspoon **cumin seeds**

Juice the oranges.

Place the carrots in a saucepan with half the orange juice, add water to cover if necessary, bring to the boil and simmer for 10 minutes. Add the cashews and apricots, cover and cook for a further 5–7 minutes until the carrots are just tender.

Meanwhile, put the cumin seeds in a frying pan and toast over a high heat for 1–2 minutes. Grind the toasted seeds briefly in a pestle and mortar.

Place the carrot mixture in a food processor or blender, add the remaining orange juice and process until smooth. Transfer to a bowl and chill for at least an hour and serve sprinkled with the ground cumin seeds.

For lemony cashew dip, soak 4 tablespoons cashew nuts in water for 2 hours to soften. Juice 1 roughly peeled lemon. Transfer the lemon juice to a food processor or blender, add the drained cashew nuts, 1 tablespoon tahini, 1 peeled garlic clove and process until smooth, gradually adding olive oil until you have the consistency you prefer.

chocolate & orange dip

Serves **2**

1 **orange**
2 tablespoons **cocoa nibs**
1 large **avocado**
½ teaspoon **honey**
apple and **pear** slices,
   to serve

Grate the rind of the orange and reserve. Roughly peel and then juice the orange.

Grind the cocoa nibs to a powder. Peel and stone the avocado.

Transfer the orange juice, cocoa powder, avocado and honey to a blender or food processor and process until smooth. Stir in the grated orange rind. Serve with slices of apple and pear.

For orange & mango dip, prepare the orange as above. Transfer the orange juice, 1 large peeled and stoned avocado, 1 large peeled and stoned mango and a 2 cm (¾ inch) piece stem ginger to a food processor or blender and process until smooth.

juicy soups

green gazpacho

Serves **4**

1 **lime**, roughly peeled
1 large **tomato**
1 **cucumber**, roughly
  chopped
1 **yellow pepper**, cored and
  deseeded
2 **garlic cloves**, chopped
1 **avocado**, peeled and
  stoned
6 **spring onions**, trimmed and
  roughly chopped
15 g (½ oz) **mint**
100 g (3½ oz) **natural yogurt**
8 **ice cubes**
2 tablespoons **extra virgin
  olive oil**
chopped **chives**, to garnish

Juice the lime with the tomato.

Transfer the juice to a food processor or blender, add the cucumber, yellow pepper, garlic, avocado, spring onions, mint and yogurt and process until nearly smooth. Chill until cold.

Ladle the soup into bowls, add a couple of ice cubes to each bowl, drizzle with extra virgin olive oil and garnish with the chopped chives.

For tomato gazpacho, juice the lime and tomato as above. Transfer the juice to a food processor or blender, add 1 roughly chopped cucumber, 1 cored and deseeded red pepper, 2 chopped garlic cloves, 6 trimmed and roughly chopped spring onions, 4 roughly chopped tomatoes, 15 g (½ oz) basil leaves and 2 tablespoons olive oil and process until nearly smooth. Chill until cold. Serve garnished with 1 peeled, stoned and diced avocado.

carrot, lentil & orange soup

Serves **4**

3 **oranges**, roughly peeled
1 teaspoon **cumin seeds**
1 teaspoon **mustard seeds**
1 teaspoon **coriander seeds**
1 **onion**, peeled and diced
250 g (8 oz) **carrots**, peeled
 and diced
75 g (3 oz) **red lentils**
600 ml (1 pint) **vegetable
 stock**
2 tablespoons **natural yogurt**
coriander sprigs, to garnish

Juice the oranges.

Dry-fry the spices in a saucepan over a medium heat for 1–2 minutes. Add the onion, carrots, red lentils, orange juice and vegetable stock, bring to the boil and simmer for 25–30 minutes until the carrots are tender and the lentils are soft.

Transfer the soup in batches to a food processor or blender and process until smooth, transferring each successive batch to a clean saucepan. Heat through gently.

Ladle the soup into bowls, top with a swirl of yogurt and garnish with coriander sprigs.

For carrot & coriander soup, make as above but increase the carrots to 300 g (10 oz) and omit the lentils. Stir 15 g (½ oz) coriander leaves into the soup before blending. Serve with natural yogurt and a sprinkling of paprika.

roasted pepper & tomato soup

Serves **2**

4 **red peppers**, cored and
   deseeded
500 g (1 lb) **tomatoes**, halved
1 teaspoon **olive oil**
1 **onion**, chopped
1 **carrot**, chopped
600 ml (1 pint) **vegetable
   stock**
2 tablespoons **crème fraîche**
handful of **basil leaves**, torn
pepper

Put the peppers, skin-side up, and the tomatoes, skin-side down, on a baking sheet under a hot grill and cook for 8–10 minutes until the skins of the peppers are blackened. Cover the peppers with damp kitchen paper, leave to cool, then remove the paper along with the skins and slice the flesh. Leave the tomatoes to cool, then remove the skins.

Heat the oil in a large saucepan, add the onion and carrot and fry for 5 minutes. Add the stock and the skinned roasted peppers and tomatoes, bring to the boil and simmer for 20 minutes until the carrot is tender.

Transfer the soup in batches to a food processor or blender and process until smooth, transferring each successive batch to a clean saucepan. Heat through gently. Stir through the crème fraîche and basil and season well with pepper.

Ladle the soup into bowls and serve.

For roasted courgette & pea soup, replace the red peppers with 4 medium courgettes, sliced lengthways and roasted as above. Add 200 g (7 oz) frozen peas with the stock and bring to the boil. Season to taste and garnish with torn basil and mint leaves.

pistou soup

Serves **4**

1 tablespoon **olive oil**
1 **onion**, peeled and diced
1 **leek**, trimmed and sliced
1 **celery stick**, diced
2 **carrots**, peeled and diced
1 small **fennel bulb**, trimmed and diced
250 g (8 oz) **celeriac**, peeled and diced
125 g (4 oz) **frozen peas**
1 x 400 g (13 oz) can **haricot beans**, drained
30 g (1¼ oz) **spinach**
4 tablespoons **pesto**
salt and **pepper**
basil leaves, to garnish

Heat the oil in a saucepan. Add the onion, leek, celery, carrots, fennel and celeriac and cook gently over a low heat for 8–10 minutes, until starting to soften but not browned. Pour over 1 litre (1¾ pints) of boiling water and season with salt and pepper. Bring to the boil and simmer for 10–15 minutes, adding the peas and beans for the last minute of cooking.

Meanwhile, juice the spinach. Pour the juice into a small bowl, add the pesto and stir to combine.

Ladle the soup into bowls, stir a spoonful of the pesto into each bowl of soup and garnish with a few basil leaves.

For winter vegetable soup, heat 1 tablespoon olive oil in a saucepan. Add 1 peeled and chopped onion, 2 trimmed and sliced leeks, 2 peeled and diced carrots, 250 g (8 oz) peeled and diced swede and 2 peeled and diced parsnips and cook gently over a low heat for 8–10 minutes, until starting to soften but not browned. Pour over 1 litre (1¾ pints) of vegetable stock, bring to the boil and simmer for 12–15 minutes. Season to taste. Juice 30 g (1¼ oz) watercress. Pour the juice into a small bowl, add 4 tablespoons of red pesto and stir to combine. Ladle the soup into bowls and stir a spoonful of the pesto into each bowl of soup.

salmon & horseradish soup

Serves **4**

1 tablespoon **olive oil**
1 **leek**, trimmed and sliced
500 g (1 lb) **potatoes**, peeled
  and chopped
1 litre (1¾ pints) **fish stock**
275 g (9 oz) **salmon fillet**, cut
  into bite-size chunks
2 tablespoons **natural yogurt**
2 cm (¾ inch) piece fresh
  horseradish root
salt and **pepper**
chopped chives, to garnish

Heat the oil in a large saucepan. Add the leek and sauté for 3–4 minutes. Then stir in the potatoes, pour in the stock, bring to the boil and simmer for 12–15 minutes until the potatoes are tender. Stir in half the salmon chunks and cook for a further 2 minutes.

Add the yogurt and stir through. Transfer the soup in batches to a food processor or blender and process until smooth, transferring each successive batch to a clean saucepan.

Juice the horseradish. Pour the juice into the soup, add the remaining salmon chunks and heat through gently. Season with salt and pepper.

Ladle the soup into bowls and garnish with some chopped chives.

For chunky salmon soup, heat 1 tablespoon olive oil in a saucepan. Add 2 trimmed and sliced leeks and sauté for 2 minutes, then add 1 large peeled and diced potato, 75 g (3 oz) red lentils and 750 ml (1 ¼ pints) skimmed milk, bring to the boil and simmer for 25–30 minutes. Stir in 200 g (7 oz) salmon fillet, cut into chunks, and cook for 2–3 minutes more. Juice 2 cm (¾ inch) fresh root ginger and stir the juice into the soup. Season to taste and serve sprinkled with chopped parsley.

bean soup with guacamole

Serves **2**

1 teaspoon **olive oil**
1 **onion**, chopped
1 **garlic clove**, crushed
1 **red chilli**, deseeded and
   chopped
1 x 400 g (13 oz) can **mixed
   beans**, rinsed and drained
220 g (7½ oz) can **chopped
   tomatoes**
300 ml (½ pint) **vegetable
   stock**
salt and **pepper**
tortilla chips, to serve

Guacamole
1 **avocado**, skinned and
   stoned
2 **spring onions**, finely sliced
2 **tomatoes**, chopped
1 tablespoon chopped
   coriander leaves
juice of ½ **lime**

Make the guacamole. Roughly chop the avocado flesh and mash it together with the spring onions, tomatoes, coriander and lime juice. Set aside.

Heat the oil in a medium saucepan. Add the onion, garlic and chilli and fry for 2–3 minutes or until softened. Add the beans, tomatoes and stock, bring to the boil and simmer for 10 minutes.

Transfer three-quarters of the soup to a food processor or blender and process until almost smooth. Add to the reserved soup and stir to combine. Season to taste with salt and pepper and heat through gently.

Serve the soup with the guacamole and tortilla chips.

For smoked bacon & bean soup with guacamole, add 50 g (2 oz) chopped smoked streaky bacon to the saucepan with the onion, garlic and chilli and cook for 2–3 minutes. Continue as above. Garnish with a spoonful of crème fraîche and serve with the guacamole.

chilled avocado & broccoli soup

Serves **4**

1 **lime**, roughly peeled
150 g (5 oz) **broccoli florets**
350 g (11½ oz) **cucumber**,
  roughly chopped
2 **garlic cloves**
2 large **avocados**, peeled
  and stoned
4 **tomatoes**
6–8 **basil leaves**
salt and **pepper**

Juice the lime with the broccoli.

Put the cucumber, garlic, avocado and half of the tomatoes and basil leaves in a food processor or blender. Pour in the juice and process until smooth, adding a little water to loosen the mixture if necessary. Season to taste and chill for at least 30 minutes before serving.

Finely chop the remaining tomatoes and basil leaves. Ladle the soup into bowls and serve sprinkled with the chopped tomatoes and basil.

For chilled cucumber soup, juice ½ lemon with 1 celery stick. Transfer the juice to a food processor or blender, add 3 cucumbers – about 1 kg (2 lb) in total, 1 red chilli (optional), a small handful of mint leaves and 3 ice cubes and process until smooth. Season to taste and serve with a drizzle of avocado oil.

chicken & sweet potato soup

Serves **2**

2 teaspoons **olive oil**
1 **small onion**, chopped
1 **garlic clove**, crushed
1 **red chilli**, deseeded and
  chopped
1 large **sweet potato**, peeled
  and cubed
1 large boneless, skinless
  chicken breast, chopped
1 x 400 g (13 oz) can
  coconut milk
600 ml (1 pint) **chicken stock**
1 tablespoon chopped
  coriander leaves
salt

Heat the oil in a nonstick frying pan. Add the onion, garlic and chilli and fry for 3 minutes until softened. Add the sweet potato and chicken and continue to fry for 2–3 minutes until the chicken is coloured all over. Add the coconut milk and stock to the pan, bring to the boil, cover and simmer for 15 minutes until the potato is tender.

Transfer the soup in batches to a food processor or blender and process until smooth, transferring each successive batch to a clean saucepan. Heat through gently. Season to taste with salt, stir through the chopped coriander and serve.

For spiced butternut squash soup, cook the onion, garlic and chilli as above, but omit the chicken and replace the sweet potato with 1 medium peeled and chopped butternut squash. Add the coconut milk and 300 ml (½ pint) vegetable stock instead of the chicken stock. Bring to the boil and finish as above.

beetroot & horseradish soup

Serves **4**

1 tablespoon **sunflower oil**
1 **red onion**, peeled and
   chopped
1 **celery stick**, chopped
1 tablespoon chopped **thyme**
500 g (1 lb) **beetroot**, peeled
   and cut into small chunks
1 tablespoon **red wine**
   vinegar
900 ml (1½ pints) hot
   vegetable stock
2 tablespoons **creamed**
   horseradish sauce, plus
   2 teaspoons
salt and **pepper**
crusty bread, to serve

To garnish
3 tablespoons **soured cream**
   or **crème fraîche**
chopped chives

Heat the oil in a large saucepan, add the onion, celery and thyme and cook gently for 3–4 minutes. Add the beetroot and vinegar and cook for 2 minutes.

Pour over the stock, cover and simmer for about 25 minutes until the beetroot is tender. Season to taste with salt and pepper and stir in 2 tablespoons of horseradish sauce.

Transfer the soup in batches to a food processor or blender and process until smooth, transferring each successive batch to a clean saucepan. Heat through gently.

Ladle the soup into bowls. Mix the soured cream or crème fraîche with the remaining horseradish sauce and spoon on top of the soup. Garnish with chopped chives and serve with crusty bread, if liked.

For beetroot & caraway soup, heat 1 tablespoon sunflower oil in a large saucepan, add 1 chopped onion and 1 crushed garlic clove and cook gently for 3–4 minutes until softened. Stir in 1 teaspoon caraway seeds, 500 g (1 lb) beetroot, peeled and diced, 1 medium potato, peeled and diced, 1 tablespoon cider vinegar and 900 ml (1½ pints) vegetable stock. Cover and simmer for 30 minutes until the beetroot and potato are tender. Season to taste with salt and pepper, then transfer the soup in batches to a food processor or blender and process until smooth, transferring each successive batch to a clean saucepan. Heat through gently. Serve topped with a spoonful of Greek yogurt and a sprinkling of caraway seeds.

broccoli & cheddar soup

Serves **2**

1 kg (2 lb) **broccoli**
1 tablespoon **olive oil**
1 **onion**, chopped
1 **large potato**, peeled and quartered
1.5 litres (2½ pints) **vegetable stock**
100 g (3½ oz) **crème fraîche**
1 tablespoon **lemon juice**
1 teaspoon **Worcestershire sauce**
a few drops of **Tabasco sauce**
125 g (4 oz) **mature Cheddar cheese**, grated
salt and **pepper**
watercress, to garnish

Remove all the tough stems and leaves from the broccoli. Cut off the stalks, peel them and cut them into 2.5 cm (1 inch) pieces. Break the florets into very small pieces and set them aside.

Heat the olive oil in a large saucepan. Add the onion and broccoli stalks and cook, covered, for 5 minutes over a medium heat, stirring frequently.

Add the broccoli florets, potato and vegetable stock to the pan. Bring the mixture to the boil, season and cook, partially covered, for 25 minutes, or until all the vegetables are soft.

Transfer the soup in batches to a food processor or blender and process until smooth, transferring each successive batch to a clean saucepan. Chill until required.

When ready to serve, add the crème fraîche, lemon juice, Worcestershire sauce and a few drops of Tabasco to the pan. Heat the soup gently and simmer for 3–5 minutes, but do not allow the soup to boil. Just before serving, stir in the grated Cheddar. Serve the soup, garnished with watercress.

For creamy cauliflower & Cheddar soup, cut 1 large cauliflower into small florets. Fry in 1 tablespoon olive oil with 1 chopped onion as above. Add 600 ml (1 pint) vegetable stock, season and simmer for 10 minutes. Purée in batches, return to the pan. Chill until required. Stir in 450 ml (¾ pint) milk, 2 teaspoons Dijon mustard and a little grated nutmeg. Reheat and stir in 75 g (3 oz) grated Cheddar.

curried parsnip soup

Serves **4**

1 tablespoon **olive oil**
1 **onion**, chopped
2 **garlic cloves**, crushed
2.5cm (1 inch) piece of fresh
   root ginger, peeled and
   chopped
1 tablespoon **medium curry
   powder**
1 teaspoon **cumin seeds**
750 g (1½ lb) **parsnips**,
   peeled and chopped
1 litre (1¾ pints) **vegetable
   stock**
salt and **pepper**

To serve
natural yogurt
2 tablespoons chopped
   coriander leaves
naan bread

Heat the olive oil in a large saucepan, add the onion, garlic and ginger and cook over a medium heat for 4–5 minutes until softened.

Stir in the curry powder and cumin seeds and cook, stirring, for 2 minutes, then stir in the parsnips, making sure that they are well coated in the spice mixture. Pour over the stock and bring to the boil, then cover and simmer for 20–25 minutes until the parsnips are tender. Season to taste with salt and pepper.

Transfer the soup in batches to a food processor or blender and process until smooth, transferring each successive batch to a clean saucepan. Heat through gently. Serve in cups with dollops of yogurt, garnished with the coriander and with warmed naan bread.

For caramelized parsnip & honey soup, heat 1 tablespoon olive oil in a flameproof roasting tin on the hob, add the peeled and chopped parsnips and 2 thyme sprigs and turn to coat in the oil. Roast in a preheated oven, 200°C (400°F), Gas Mark 6, for 30–35 minutes, stirring once, until golden brown. Stir in 2 tablespoons clear honey and roast for a further 10 minutes until the parsnips have caramelized. Transfer to a saucepan, stir in 1 litre (1¾ pints) vegetable stock and bring to the boil on the hob, then simmer for 10 minutes. Transfer to a food processor or blender, in batches, and process until smooth. Return to the pan, season to taste and stir in 300 ml (½ pint) boiling water, then bring back to the boil. Serve in bowls with crusty bread.

potato & smoked garlic soup

Serves **4**

1 tablespoon **olive oil**

1 **large onion**, sliced

2 smoked **garlic cloves**, crushed

750 g (1½ lb) **floury potatoes**, peeled and cut into small cubes

1 litre (1¾ pints) **vegetable stock**

½ teaspoon **smoked sea salt**

125 ml (4 fl oz) **milk**

4 tablespoons **fresh herbs**, such as parsley, thyme and chives, plus extra snipped chives, to garnish

pepper

Greek yogurt, to serve

Heat the olive oil in a large saucepan, add the onion and smoked garlic and cook over a medium heat for 3–4 minutes until softened. Stir in the potatoes, cover and cook for 5 minutes.

Add the stock and season with the smoked sea salt and pepper. Bring to the boil, then reduce the heat, cover and simmer for 30 minutes until the potatoes are tender.

Transfer the soup in batches to a food processor or blender and process until smooth, transferring each successive batch to a clean saucepan. Stir in the milk and herbs and reheat gently.

Ladle the soup into bowls, add a spoonful of Greek yogurt and garnish with chives and pepper.

For smoked sweet potato soup, cook the onion and garlic as above, then add 1 tablespoon smoked paprika and cook, stirring, for 1 minute. Stir in 300 g (10 oz) potato and 450 g (1 lb) sweet potato, both peeled and cut into small cubes, and cook for 5 minutes. Add the stock as above and bring to the boil, then cover and simmer for 30 minutes until the potato is tender. Blend as above until smooth, then serve with a spoonful of Greek yogurt, garnished with a sprinkling of smoked paprika and freshly snipped chives.

tomato & chorizo soup

Serves **2**

500 g (1 lb) **red peppers**,
  cored and deseeded
2 tablespoons **olive oil**
1 **large onion**, chopped
2 **garlic cloves**, crushed
150 g (5 oz) **chorizo**
  sausage, sliced
1 teaspoon ground **cumin**
1 teaspoon **smoked paprika**
500 g (1 lb) **tomatoes**, halved
  and deseeded
600 ml (1 pint) **chicken** or
  vegetable stock
handful of **parsley**, chopped
salt and **pepper**

Put the red peppers on a baking sheet, and drizzle over half the olive oil. Place in a preheated oven 200°C (400°F), Gas Mark 6 for 10–15 minutes, turning after 5 minutes.

Heat the remaining olive oil in a large saucepan, while the peppers are roasting, add the onion, garlic and chorizo and fry for 3–4 minutes until the onion is softened and the chorizo is beginning to brown. Stir in the spices and fry for a further minute.

Add the tomatoes and the stock to the saucepan and season well. Bring to the boil and simmer for 5 minutes.

Remove the red peppers from the oven, skin then roughly chop them and add to the soup and simmer for a further 15 minutes. Remove from the heat and allow to cool for 5 minutes.

Transfer the soup in batches to a food processor or blender and roughly blend, transferring each successive batch to a clean saucepan. Heat through gently, then stir in the parsley and serve.

For tomato soup with creamy basil, omit the red peppers and fry the onion and garlic as above, replacing the chorizo and spices with 1 chopped carrot and 1 chopped celery stick. Add the tomatoes and vegetable stock, bring to the boil and simmer for 25 minutes. Transfer the soup in batches to a food processor or blender and process until smooth, transferring each successive batch to a clean saucepan. Heat through gently and stir in 2 tablespoons mascarpone cheese and 1 tablespoon pesto. Season and serve.

bacon & white bean soup

Serves **4**

1 teaspoon **olive oil**

2 lean **smoked bacon rashers**, chopped

2 **garlic cloves**, crushed

1 **onion**, chopped

a few **thyme** or **lemon thyme sprigs**

2 x 400 g (13 oz) cans **cannellini beans**, drained and rinsed

900 ml (1½ pints) **vegetable stock**

2 tablespoons chopped **parsley**

pepper

Heat the oil in a large saucepan, add the bacon, garlic and onion and fry for 3–4 minutes until the bacon is beginning to brown and the onion to soften.

Add the thyme and fry for a further 1 minute. Add the beans and stock to the pan and bring to the boil, then reduce the heat and simmer for 10 minutes.

Transfer the soup in batches to a food processor or blender with the parsley and pepper and process until smooth, transferring each successive batch to a clean saucepan. Heat through gently and serve.

For herb & white bean crostini, to serve as an accompaniment, lightly mash a drained 400 g (13 oz) can cannellini beans and then combine with 2 tablespoons each of finely chopped basil and parsley, 1 crushed garlic clove, a pinch of dried chilli flakes and 50 g (2 oz) chopped cherry tomatoes. Toast 8 thin slices of baguette and top with the herby bean mixture.

green detox soup

Serves **4**

1 tablespoon **coconut oil**
1 large **onion**, peeled and
  chopped
1 **leek**, trimmed and sliced
2 **garlic cloves**, crushed
2 cm (¾ inch) piece fresh **root
  ginger**, peeled and diced
1 teaspoon **cumin seeds**
½ teaspoon ground **turmeric**
150 g (5 oz) **Savoy cabbage**
150 g (5 oz) **broccoli florets**
1 **parsnip**, peeled and
  chopped
900 ml (1½ pints) **vegetable
  stock**
1 **lemon**
50 g (2 oz) **spinach**
salt and **pepper**
2 tablespoons **natural yogurt**
chopped **coriander leaves**

Heat the oil in a large saucepan, add the onion and leek and sauté for 4–5 minutes. Stir in the garlic, ginger and spices and cook for 1–2 minutes, then stir in the cabbage, broccoli and parsnip and cook for a further 1 minute. Add the stock, bring to the boil and simmer for 12–15 minutes, until the parsnip is soft.

Transfer the soup in batches to a food processor or blender and process until smooth, transferring each successive batch to a clean saucepan.

Juice the lemon with the spinach. Stir the juice into the soup and season to taste. Heat through gently, if necessary.

Ladle the soup into bowls and top with a dollop of natural yogurt and sprinkling of chopped coriander.

For creamy kale detox soup, heat 1 tablespoon coconut oil in a large saucepan. Add 1 peeled and chopped onion, 1 crushed garlic clove, 2 cm (¾ inch) piece peeled and diced fresh root ginger and ½ teaspoon turmeric and sauté for 4–5 minutes. Stir in 2 peeled and diced carrots and 175 g (6 oz) chopped kale. Pour in 1 x 400 g (13 oz) can coconut milk, the juice of 75 g (3 oz) spinach leaves and 200 ml (7 fl oz) water, bring to the boil and simmer for 12–15 minutes. Season to taste and serve sprinkled with chopped chives.

strawberry & melon soup

Serves **4**

2 **oranges**, roughly peeled
1 **lemon**, roughly peeled
1 small **cantaloupe melon**,
  peeled, deseeded and cut
  into chunks
300 g (10 oz) **strawberries**,
  hulled
1 teaspoon **honey** (optional)
2 tablespoons **natural yogurt**
2 tablespoon chopped **mint**

Juice the oranges with the lemon.

Transfer the juice to a food processor or blender, add the melon and strawberries and process until smooth. Taste for sweetness and stir in the honey if necessary. Chill for at least 1 hour, stirring in half the chopped mint 20 minutes before serving.

Ladle the soup into bowls, top with a dollop of natural yogurt and sprinkle with the remaining chopped mint.

For warm berry soup, juice 6 apples. Pour the juice into a saucepan and add 300 g (10 oz) assorted fresh berries, 1 cinnamon stick and 2 cloves. Bring to the boil and simmer gently for 10 minutes. Process half the soup in a blender or food processor until smooth. Pour the processed soup back into the saucepan and stir into the remaining soup. Ladle the soup into bowls and serve with a dollop of natural yogurt.

index

acknowledgements

Commissioning editor: Eleanor Maxfield
Editor: Pollyanna Poulter
Design manager: Jaz Bahra
Designer: Tracy Killick
Production controller: Sarah Kramer

Octopus Publishing Group Octopus Publishing Group
Stephen Conroy 9 above, 16, 70, 128, 213, 217; Vanessa
Davies 101, 123; Janine Hosegood 105, 113, 61, 63, 65,
73, 79, 109, 121, 125, 131, 143, 157, 167, 173, 174, 200,
207; William Reavell 177; William Shaw 9 below, 10, 161,
171, 219, 223, 225, 227, 229; Ian Wallace 221. Shutterstock
Evgeny Karandaev 11; Kesu 12; lola1960 13; Odua Images
15; Sabino Parente 14.